Thanks for helpful hints:

Peter - chief editor
Shannon - business consultant
Dee - technical production manager
Pete - web site creator

Inspired by 30 years Head Start teaching

IAMBE'

Dedicated to all pre-school teachers

Modeled after Tiffany and our Head Start Class

Copyright @ C. May Scott

2016   www.IAMBEPRESS.com

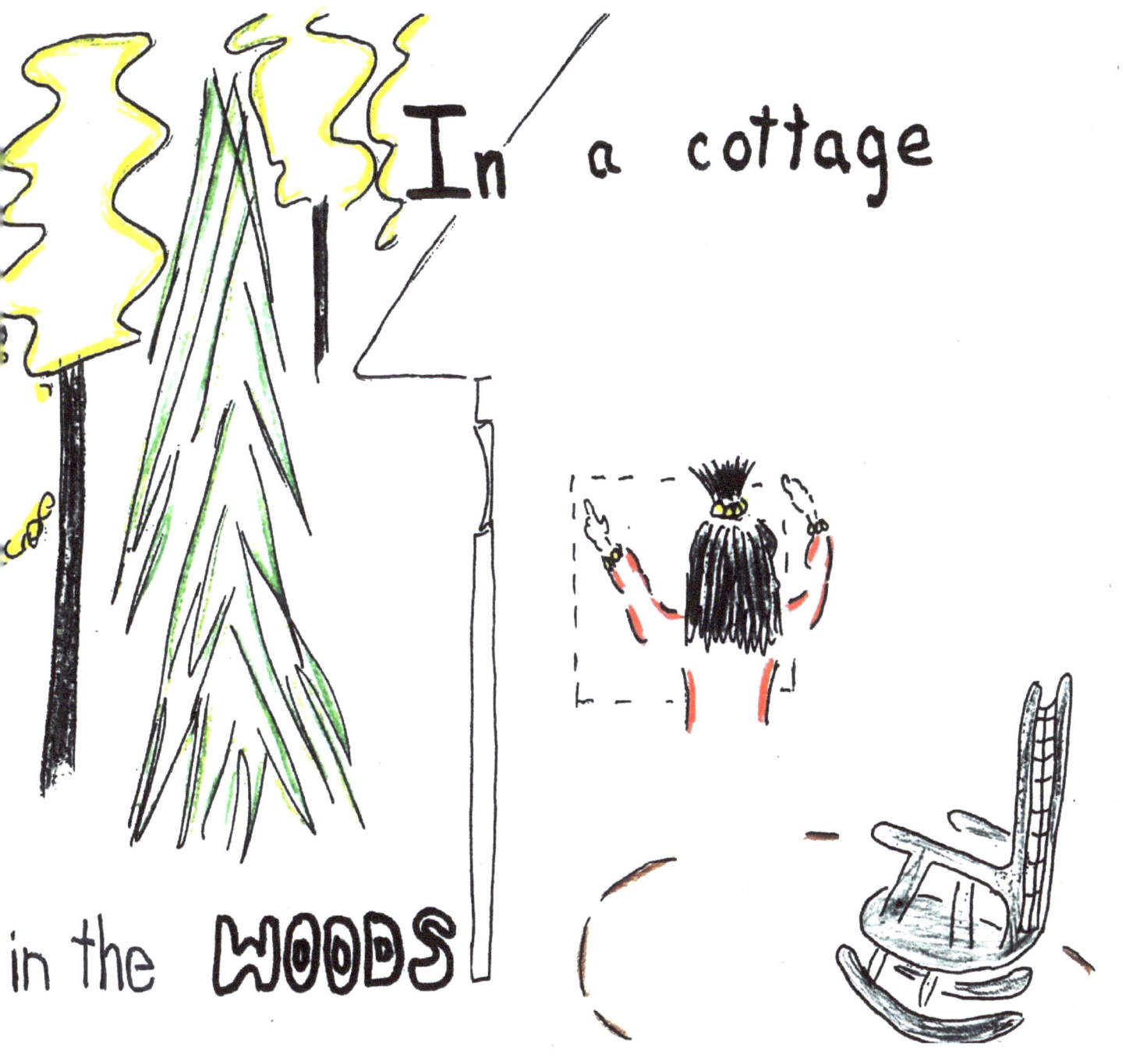

KNOCKING at the DOOR

KNOCK   Knock   Knock

BANG

i BANG KNOCK

KNOCK   KNOCK

HELP ME
HELP ME
HELP ME QUICK!

A cleaner place Begins with ME!

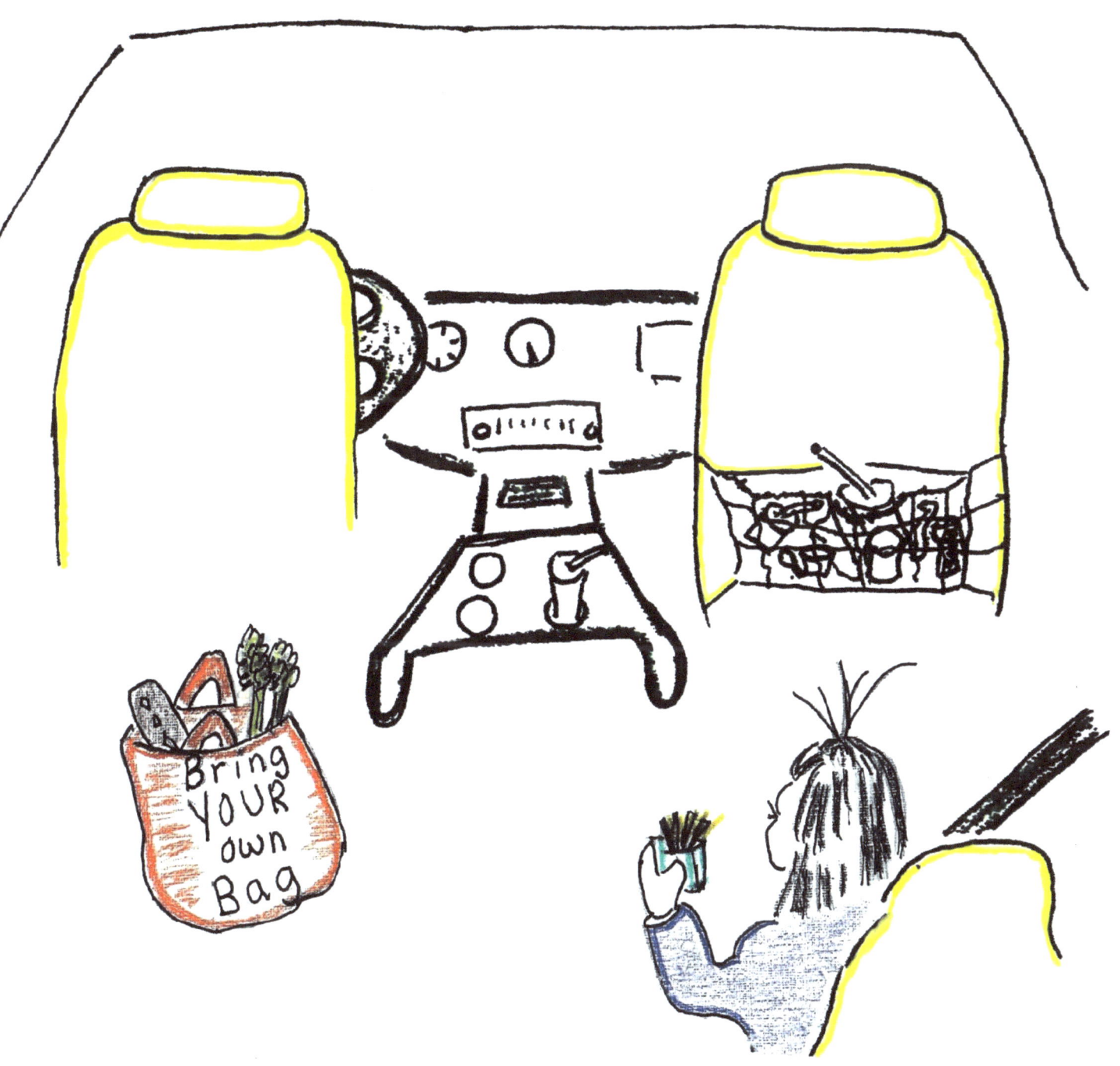

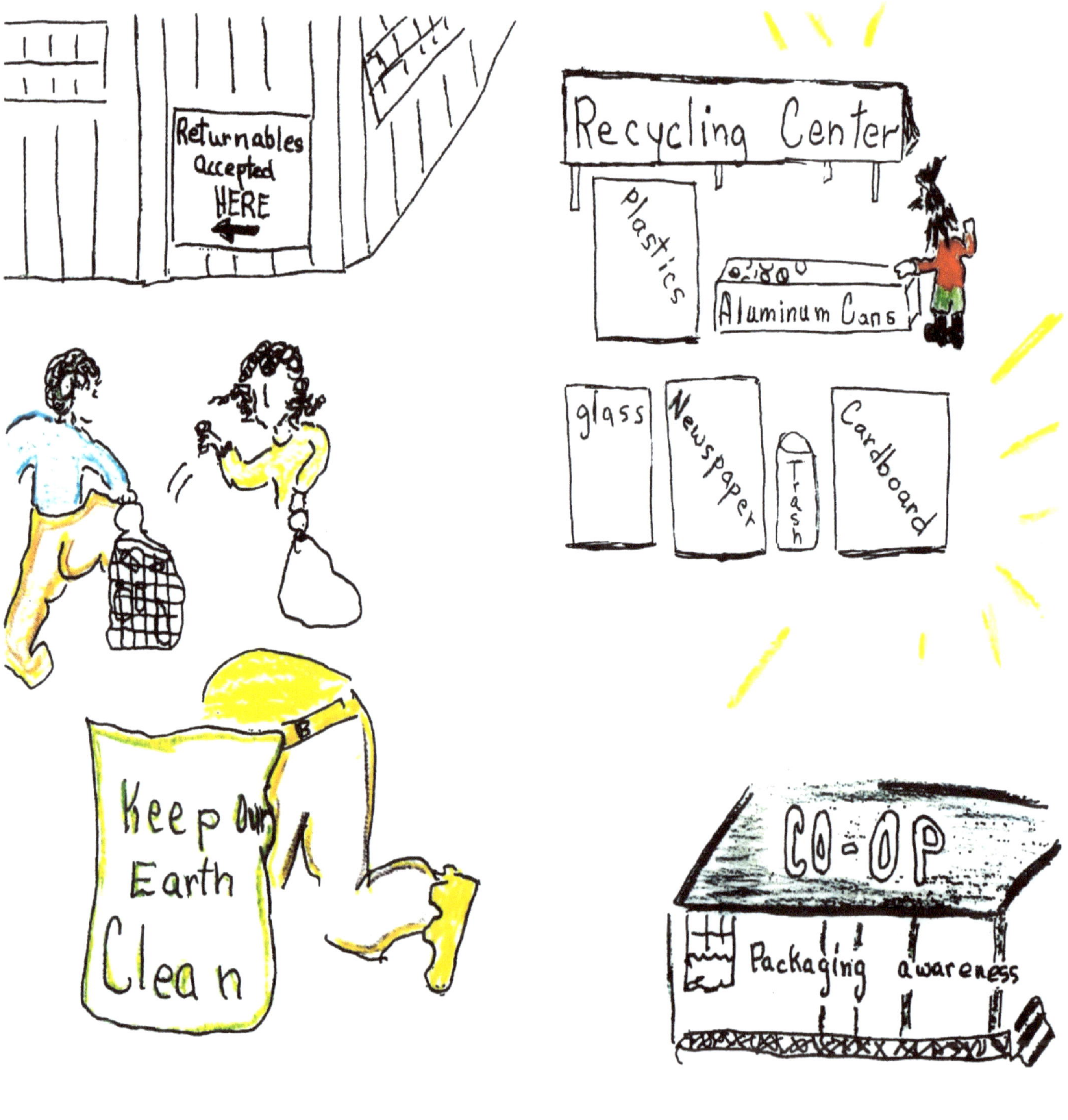
Returnables accepted HERE
Recycling Center
plastics
Aluminum Cans
glass
Newspaper
Trash
Cardboard
Keep Our Earth Clean
CO-OP
Packaging awareness

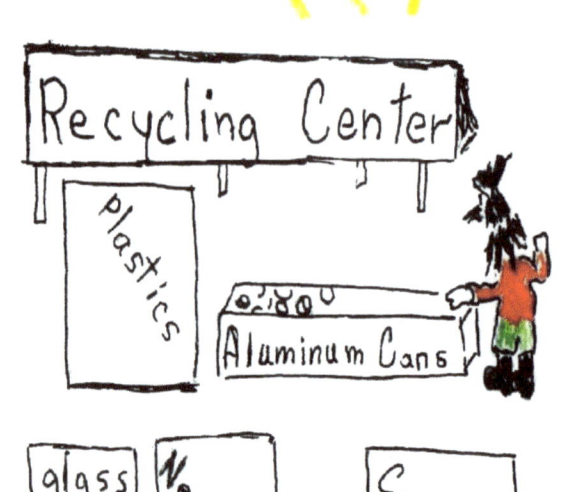

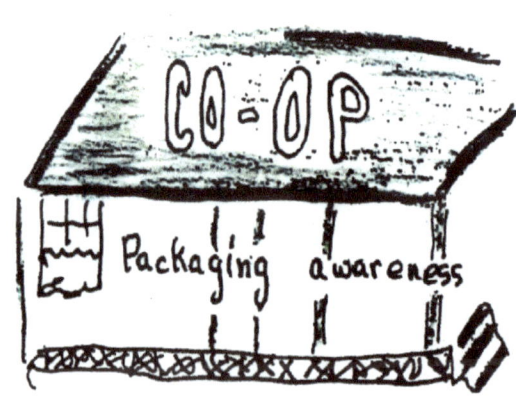

Cat

Signing
Animals

From The Book
The Joy of Signing

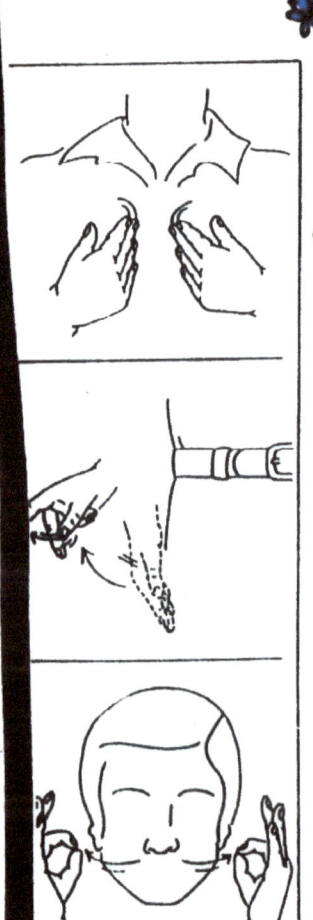

ANIMAL

Place the fingertips on the chest and rock the hands back and forth with the tips still resting on the chest.
Origin: Represents the breathing motion of an animal.
Usage: The children enjoyed the *animals* in the zoo.

DOG

Pat the leg and snap the fingers.
Origin: Imitating the natural motion of calling a dog.
Usage: a boy and his *dog*.

CAT

Place the "F" hands at the sides of the mouth and draw out to the sides.
Origin: Represents the cat's whiskers.
Usage: Siamese *cat*.

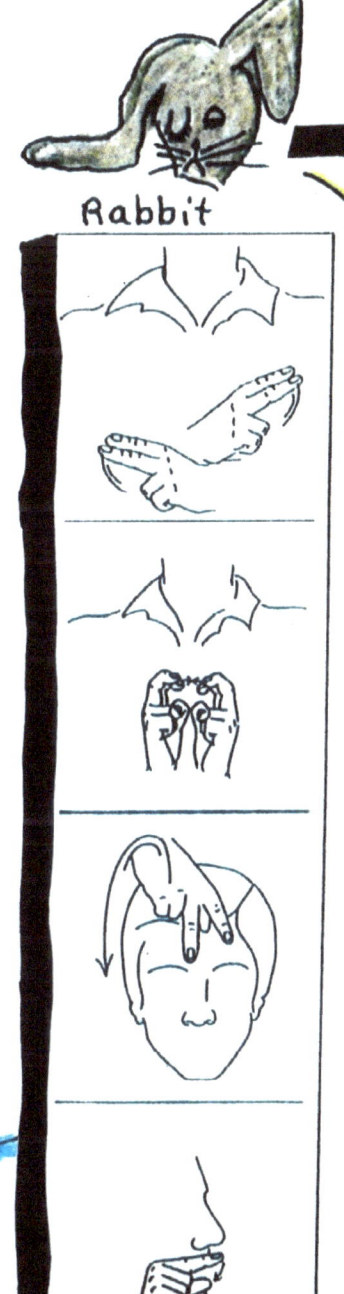

RABBIT

Place the right "H" on the left "H" crosswise; move "H" fingers back and forth several times.
Origin: Representing the ears of the rabbit.
Usage: a white *rabbit* with pink eyes.

SQUIRREL

Strike the tips of the bent "V" hands together in from you several times.
Origin: Indicates a sitting squirrel with front paws up
Usage: *Squirrels* can do damage in the house.

SKUNK

Draw the right "K" hand back over the head, beginning at the forehead.
Origin: Indicates the white stripe of the skunk.
Usage: *Skunks* know how to keep people away.

BIRD

Place the index finger and thumb in front of the mouth representing the bill; flap the arms. (The latter part is often omitted.)
Origin: The bird's bill and wings.
Usage: *Birds* fly south in the winter.

SNAKE

Use the right "G" hand pointing forward and move it forward in a circular motion, passing under the left arm.
Origin: Indicating the crawling movement.
Usage: bitten by a poisonous *snake*.

OWL

Place the "O" hands in front of the eyes so that the eyes see through the circle of the "O"; twist them toward the center several times.
Origin: The large eyes of the owl.
Usage: a wise old *owl*.

WORM

Place the right index finger on the left palm and wiggle it as it moves forward.
Origin: Represents the worm crawling.
Usage: a can of *worms*.

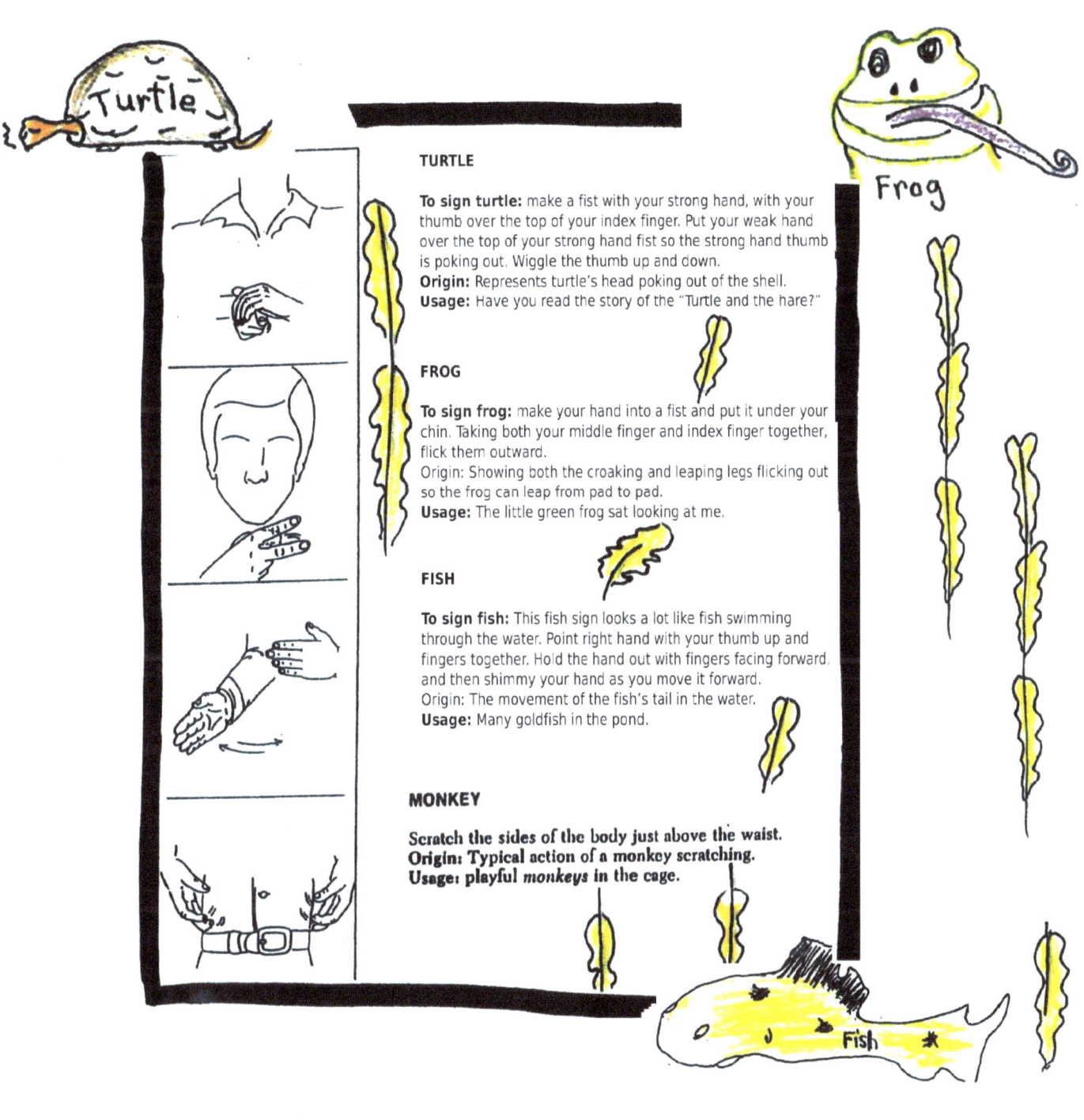

TURTLE

To sign turtle: make a fist with your strong hand, with your thumb over the top of your index finger. Put your weak hand over the top of your strong hand fist so the strong hand thumb is poking out. Wiggle the thumb up and down.
Origin: Represents turtle's head poking out of the shell.
Usage: Have you read the story of the "Turtle and the hare?"

FROG

To sign frog: make your hand into a fist and put it under your chin. Taking both your middle finger and index finger together, flick them outward.
Origin: Showing both the croaking and leaping legs flicking out so the frog can leap from pad to pad.
Usage: The little green frog sat looking at me.

FISH

To sign fish: This fish sign looks a lot like fish swimming through the water. Point right hand with your thumb up and fingers together. Hold the hand out with fingers facing forward, and then shimmy your hand as you move it forward.
Origin: The movement of the fish's tail in the water.
Usage: Many goldfish in the pond.

MONKEY

Scratch the sides of the body just above the waist.
Origin: Typical action of a monkey scratching.
Usage: playful *monkeys* in the cage.

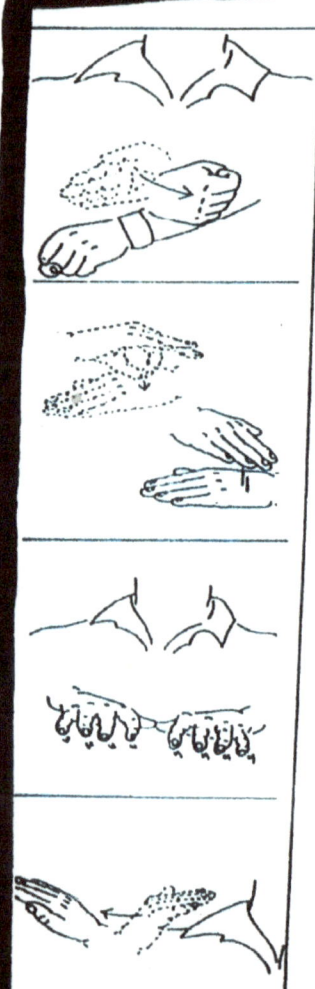

FLY

Use the right hand to catch an imaginary fly on the left forearm.
Usage: that awful *fly*.

MOSQUITO

Touch the back of the left hand with the tips of the thumb and index (in the "NINE" position); then slap the hand.
Origin: Indicating the bite and the killing of the mosquito.
Usage: many *mosquitoes* near the water.

INSECT

Touch the thumbtips of the bent "FIVE" hands together, palms down; wiggle the bent fingers, working them like a crawling insect.
Origin: The movement of the crawling insect.
Usage: afraid of all *insects*.

WINGS

Place the fingertips of the right hand on the right shoulder, draw them away and then turn the hands so the fingertips point away from the body.
Origin: Wings extending from the shoulder.
Usage: large *wings* of an eagle.

The Beginning

This is a contemporary look at our local environmental distress issues, and what action an individual child can take to turn things around. For over fifteen years, this hand-action song has been requested often by my Head Start preschoolers. This experience has encouraged me to transcribe this entertaining and important message.

About the author & illustrator

An Associate degree in Early Childhood Development gave me observational skills. Over twenty eight years of Head Start classroom experience, has shown me what works with children. And Motherhood continues to teach me right into Grandmotherhood, how to relate to the world around me.

www.ingramcontent.com/pod-product-compliance
Lightning Source LLC
Chambersburg PA
CBHW061402090426
42743CB00002B/111